HUMMER

The Next Generation

Michael Green

MBI Publishing Company

TO MY GOOD FRIEND BRENDA C. MARKIN
WHOSE SUPPORT THROUGHOUT THE RESEARCH ON THIS BOOK
HELPED ME FINISH THIS PROJECT.

First published in 1995 by MBI Publishing Company, PO Box 1, 729 Prospect Avenue, Osceola, WI 54020-0001 USA

The information in this book is true and complete to the best of our knowledge. All recommendations are made without any guarantee on the part of the author or Publisher, who also disclaim any liability incurred in connection with the use of this data or specific details.

We recognize that some words, model names and designations, for example, mentioned herein are the property of the trademark holder. We use them for identification purposes only. This is not an official publication.

MBI Publishing Company books are also available at discounts in bulk quantity for industrial or sales-promotional use. For details write to Special Sales Manager at Motorbooks International Wholesalers & Distributors, 729 Prospect Avenue, PO Box 1, Osceola, WI 54020-0001 USA.

Library of Congress Cataloging-in-Publication Data
    Green, Michael.
        Hummer, the next generation/Michael Green.
        p. cm.—(MBI Publishing Company enthusiast color series)
        ISBN 0-7603-0045-3 (pbk.)
        1. Hummer (All terrain vehicle) 2. Motor vehicles– Off road operation. I. Title. II. Series: Enthusiast color series.
TL235.6.G74   1995
629.22'042—dc20   95-34195

On the front cover: Improvements to the civilian Hummer that began with the 1994 production models included enhanced heating and air conditioning systems. Other new standard features on the 1994 models were power door locks, 124 amp alternator, improved window glass that reduces heat build-up inside the vehicle, a glove box, one piece wheels, and flow-through ventilation. Options included power windows and remote keyless entry. *AM General*

On the frontispiece: The power of the civilian Hummer is well portrayed in this great shot of veteran racer Rod Hall's vehicle taking to the air during part of the 1993 Baja 1000 race. This grueling 501-mile cross-country race in Mexico's desert provided mile after mile of the toughest terrain on earth with which to test the Hummer. Rod Hall's Hummer finished first in its class, with a time of thirteen hours thirty-three minutes. Rod Hall operates a racing school out of the Reno, Nevada, area from mid-March through early November. *AM General*

On the title page: To help prove how durable and dependable Hummers can be, AM General developed two modified civilian vehicles that were entered into the grueling fifty-six-day London to Peking Motoring Challenge in 1990. During this event, the two Hummers traveled over 9,000 miles across nine countries and two continents without a hitch. *AM General*

On the back cover: For serious off-roading–when you need to get up that hill, across that rough patch of ground, or through the snow–there's only one 4x4. The Hummer will muscle its way through 2 ft of snow. With the Hummer's lockable internal differential, it's possible to put equal power to all four wheels when added traction is needed, such as on snow-covered roads or muddy trails. *AM General*

Printed in China

Contents

Acknowledgments

Special thanks for help in putting this book together are due to: Timothy M. Bonadies, Bennie P. Brown, Ed Butkera, Susan Carney, Suzanne Curry, Kim Fogus, C. John Linarello, Bill Nahmens, Greg Stewart, Kim Wilkeson, and both AM General and the O'Gara-Hess & Eisenhardt Armoring Company.

Introduction

The popularity of sport-utility vehicles (sport-utes) and the proliferation of manufacturers who are trying to market them to the public is ever-growing. However, there still exists an incredible gap between the off-road capabilities of the many civilian-designed sport-utes and the true off-road abilities that modern manufacturing technology can provide. The only sport-ute on the civilian market today that truly represents the culmination of off-road technology is the AM General Corporation's well-known HUMMER.

The Hummer was previously called HUMVEE, which came from HMMWV, an acronym for the the US Army's High Mobility Multipurpose Wheeled Vehicle. Both HUMMER and HUMVEE are registered trademarks of AM General.

The Hummer owes its off-road abilities not to the very tame demands of the civilian marketplace but to the overwhelming requirements of the United States armed forces. In the late 1970s, the American military machine decided that it needed a fleet of newer and more capable off-road vehicles. The US armed forces wanted a tough and versatile vehicle that could perform anywhere in the world under the most extreme conditions of weather and terrain. In contrast to a sport-ute designed only for a Sunday drive on a country road or getting through to the ski lodge on a snowy night, this off-road vehicle had to transport both American soldiers and their weapons and equipment to places where the biggest threat is not just the terrain but an armed and dangerous opponent.

AM General's combat proven Hummer has performed under the world's toughest battlefield conditions and come out a winner. For those who desire only the best in off-road capabilities, the sport-ute to have is the civilian Hummer.

CHAPTER 1

Hummer History

Willys-Overland Motors (a distant ancestor of the AM General Corporation) entered the field of tactical truck development in 1940 by designing and manufacturing a prototype for America's first four-wheel drive, 1/4 ton general purpose truck. Often referred to by its initials GP, it wasn't long before GIs had found a neat new nickname for the versatile vehicle: "jeep."

Officially designated the MA-MB series, the Jeep quickly became one of the Army's most important tactical vehicles during World War II.

This was the beginning of AM General's leadership in the design and production of military wheeled vehicles. When the Korean war came along, AM General was asked to build an improved model of the Jeep. The result was the M38 series, of which more than 150,000 units were built.

The M151 Jeep was designed by Kaiser and built by both Ford and AM General as a replacement for the postwar M38 Jeep. Production began in 1964. As the years went on, the M151 family of vehicles was modified and improved to become the MI51A1 and later the M151A2 series. Pictured is an AM General-built M151A2 vehicle in its final configuration. *US Army*

The M38 later became the standard for the military forces of the U.S., the nations belonging to NATO, and other Allied nations.

For the Korean conflict, the company also produced 5,000 M170 front line ambulances by extending the basic body and chassis of the M38A1 to accommodate litters.

The history of the Hummer vehicle began in 1979 with a competition for the development of a vehicle to meet the U.S. Army's highest standards for a High Mobility Multipurpose Wheeled Vehicle (HMMWV). As that development race began, both Teledyne and Chrysler Defense, which was later sold to General Dynamics, already had HMMWV designs on their drawing boards. The proposed Chrysler vehicle was an adapted version of the Saluki desert design, while its Teledyne counterpart sprang from the design of a vehicle known as the Cheetah. Though AM General appeared to be well behind the others, the company moved into this competition with no preconceived design notions, rolled up its sleeves, and soon created an original: the Hummer.

As the largest builder of military trucks outside the Soviet Union, AM General faced the exhaustive Army testing and evaluation with a great deal of confidence. Even before the Army had formally issued its design specifications, AM General engineers had designed and built a test bed vehicle which was quietly tested at their own facility. They racked up over 17,000 miles of testing on this vehicle.

In February 1981, the Army released its specifications and requested proposals from industry. AM General moved quickly. They built five engineering prototypes and began running them through extensive and repetitive testing at

The world's best known 4x4 vehicle, the original WW2 era American-built Jeep has long since passed its prime and now is considered a collector's item by most. This beautifully restored WW2 era Jeep in Australian military colors was seen at a military vehicle collector's rally.

Because the M151 had such different handling characteristics from its predecessors it proved to be a real challenge for many soldiers' driving skills. In particular, the independent swingarm-type rear suspension provided little feedback to the driver of vehicle dynamics. When the vehicle was pushed to its limits, there was a tendency for tire "tuck-under." This MI51A2 is crewed by US Army National Guard MPs.

the Nevada Automotive Test Center, a privately-owned facility near Carson City. These vehicles were driven more than 50,000 miles while AM General sought to simulate the testing that the Army would later initiate.

Coincidentally, an additional eleven vehicles were constructed for the Army's Phase I durability and operational testing (DT/OT) where the vehicles eventually logged more than 100,000 miles.

It was expected that design flaws and manufacturing problems would surface during this phase of testing. Thus, it came as no surprise to AM General or to the Army that there were some problems with the early versions of the Hummer. The fuel system leaked, the brakes malfunctioned and the brake pads wore excessively, tire life needed improvement, and problems were encountered with the power steering. As in any such development program, engineers quickly determined suitable "fixes" for these problems, and the corrective actions were approved by the Army. When AM General submitted its production

By 1969, and the appearance of the M151A2, the tuck-under problem was corrected with a redesigned rear independent suspension system. This modification improved the M151's handling characteristics, but due to the vehicle's basic narrow width and high ground clearance for cross-country performance, vehicle stability under some conditions left much to be desired. The small size of the M151 Jeep is apparent in this US Army picture from the early 1970s.

proposal to the Army in November 1982, the proposal contained design modifications to correct all the deficiencies which had been uncovered during the DT/OT programs.

Components of the new vehicle were thoroughly analyzed in over 450 individual tests designed to prove that each part met the Army's rigid specifications. For example, twenty-seven

The entire M151 series of vehicles saw widespread service with the American armed forces. Unfortunately, the vehicle was still too small and light to fulfill all the military needs for cross-country transport of troops and equipment. This M151, shown during a US Army training exercise in the early 1970s, is mounting an 106mm recoilless rifle which is just about to be fired. *US Army*

separate tests were conducted in the crew compartment to check out operator controls and accessories. The engines were required to pass muster on 146 specific check list items, and the brakes were thoroughly examined on almost forty separate criteria. The drivetrain (consisting of the engine, transmission, transfer case, propshaft, control arms, and hubs) was subjected to twenty-nine grueling examinations.

After AM General engineers completed these individual tests and certified that the components met or exceeded the required specifications, Army

By the late 1970s, the US Army had become unhappy with the performance of civilian trucks modified for military use and its existing fleet of specially-built tactical vehicles. What was needed was a new jack-of-all-trades vehicle that could fulfill a wide range of mission requirements.

Pictured is a M561 Gamma Goat, one of the specially-designed tactical vehicles which proved unsuccessful in field use and pushed the US Army to look for something both more versatile and reliable. *US Army* testers took over. Twelve pre-production model Hummers (four TOW carriers, seven cargo/troop carriers, and one armament carrier) were delivered to the Army in the summer of 1984.

The vehicles were divided into two categories for the durability and performance testing that was to follow. Four Hummers were assigned to durability testing and three for the European-style performance phase, and at a desert training center two Hummers were slated for durability testing, three for performance testing.

Durability testing, or DT as it is called, began on July 1 with two shifts of drivers and support personnel pushing the Hummers to their design

In 1979, the US Army created a written requirement for an High Mobility Multipurpose Wheeled Vehicle (HMMWV). It was looking for a single vehicle that could perform the roles of many different vehicles then in military service. Pictured is one of AM General's early HMMWV prototype vehicles that went through the Army's grueling tests. This particular vehicle is configured as a weapons carrier. *AM General*

limits sixteen hours a day. The goal was to put 20,000 miles on each of the DT vehicles during the ensuing five months. The vehicles were driven over all sorts of road surfaces in all kinds of weather. The purpose of the DT was quite simple: would the Hummer stand up to the kind of rough treatment that it would later receive in a combat unit? A second purpose of the DT was to determine the Hummer's ease of maintenance. How difficult would it be for troops in the field to service and make minor repairs on the vehicles? What would it take to change a tire, or replace a

Since HMMWV was a mouthful to pronounce every time they wanted to talk about the vehicle, American soldiers called it the Humvee. AM General later decided to call it the Hummer, which does not stand for anything in particular. Both names are registered trademarks of AM General. Pictured is a US Army Hummer mounting a TOW Missile Launcher during a desert training exercise. *Greg Stewart*

belt, or repair a radiator? How often would routine maintenance need to be performed? The all-important answer to be determined was: would the Hummer meet or exceed the Army's tough MMBMF (Mean Miles Between Mission Failure) requirements or not?

During the performance testing, the Hummers were checked for such factors as acceleration, weight distribution, cold temperature starting, fuel consumption, electromagnetic interference, and similar design criteria. Vehicles were air-dropped, slung under helicopters, carried inside other huge helicopters and off-loaded from low flying transport planes using the Low Altitude Parachute Extraction System (LAPES). They were driven at high temperatures in Death Valley and over torturous mountain roads in Pennsylvania. They were towed by wreckers and, in turn, were used to tow other simulated disabled vehicles. Live firing demonstrations were conducted from Hummers employing the TOW antiarmor missile, 40mm grenade launcher, 7.62mm machine gun, and .50 caliber machine gun.

While the Hummers were being tested at Aberdeen and Yuma, five additional pre-production models were delivered to Fort Hunter-Liggett, California, early in September. Following a short driver training program, the five vehicles began what was officially described as the Follow-on Test and Evaluation (Phase II) on September 24. Unlike the testing at the two proving grounds, the FOT&E was conducted by soldiers who were not professional drivers or test evaluators. This program combined aspects of both the durability and performance testing. The goals were to accumulate lots of mileage in a relatively brief time, but also to perform additional specific performance testing. More checking of the Hummer's adaptability for air mobility was done. Refueling times were measured, and the Hummer's unique run-flat tires were evaluated. A human factors safety assessment was accomplished. Most importantly,

Looking into a US Army Hummer from the driver's side, you first notice the vehicle's large drivetrain housing which divides the vehicle's crew compartment in half. The drivetrain's midship position allows the Hummer's front differential to be raised much further into the vehicle's frame than any other types of 4x4 currently in use. Another thing you notice right away is the Spartan appearance of the vehicle's interior. Creature comforts are non-existent in military Hummers.

the Army's demanding RAM-D (Reliability, Availability, Maintainability, and Durability) standards were applied.

The Phase II FOT&E was completed satisfactorily and on schedule November 1. The five vehicles had passed individual performance testing and had accumulated 30,867 miles against the goal of 25,000 miles during the five-and-a-half week period. Each vehicle was driven more than 5,800 miles.

There is little in external appearance that would allow the causal observer to distinguish between the various types of basic Hummer models. Generally, improvements to US military Hummers have been confined to unseen interior changes. The Hummer pictured is a M998 Cargo/Troop Carrier. *AM General*

FOT&E continued in mid-November at two widely separated locations. Phase IIIa involving three Hummers was conducted at Fort Knox, Kentucky. Here, European terrain was simulated as the vehicles were involved in such operations as driving in mud and towing heavy trailers. A total of more than 3,000 miles of testing was accumulated. In California, at the Naval Amphibious Base Coronado, the U.S. Marine Corps tested two vehicles (Phase IIIb) for compatibility with the amphibious environment. Deep water fording involved driving a Hummer in water sixty inches deep. Shipboard compatibility tests and 1,200 miles of beach mobility tests were conducted by the Marines, and the vehicles were closely examined for corrosion problems.

During Operation Desert Shield ,American soldiers were so impressed with the Hummer's outstanding mobility over all types of terrain, that they started to refer to the Hummer as the "son of Jeep" or "a Jeep on steroids." With a bare minimum of maintenance and heavily overloaded, even by US military standards, AM General's Hummer proved to be a mechanically superior vehicle that nothing could stop. *US Army*

The Army's test phase was scheduled over a five month period, after which a call for production proposals would be made from the competing contractors. AM General took in stride the fact that its Hummers were the first vehicles to complete the durability testing. The company also came through the rigorous testing with the lightest vehicles and high performance ratings. Clearly, the Hummer had scored as the superior technical offering.

On March 22, 1983, the U.S. Army Tank-Automotive Command awarded to AM General a $1.2 billion contract to produce 55,000 Hummers. These were to be delivered in fifteen different

Pictured under a camouflage net at Camp Roberts, California, this US Army Hummer has a pair of small smoke generator units mounted on its rear cargo bay. Smoke has a variety of uses on the modern battlefield. In the attack, it can conceal vehicles, deceiving the enemy as to the strength and location of the attacking forces. In the defense, it can confuse, slow, and blind attacking elements and conceal defensive positions and movements.

configurations over a five year period. The contract included an option to increase the number of vehicles purchased by 100% during each of the five option years. The Army has since exercised options on additional Hummers, raising the total contract order to 100,000 vehicles. It was the largest multi-year contract for tactical vehicles ever awarded by the U.S. Army.

When it was first produced by AM General, the Hummer was officially known as the Hummer M998 model and product improvements have resulted in the production of an Hummer M998A1 and M998A2 model vehicles. This technologically advanced 1 1/4-ton, 4x4, multipurpose vehicle answered the U.S. armed forces' need for superior mobility in a tactical field environment. It is exceptionally versatile, mobile, fast, and replaced an assortment of armed forces vehicles, including the M151 Jeep, M274s Mule, M561 Gama Goat, and some M880s trucks.

As the centerpiece of the Army's force modernization program, the Hummer had to be air transportable, maintainable, reliable, and survivable. The Hummer met all those requirements,

The US Army's CH-47 medium-lift Chinook helicopter has both the engine power and internal cargo space to carry at least one military Hummer (not all models) when needed. Pictured in Gembach, Germany, during the early stages of Operation Desert Shield is a Hummer being driven backwards into the cargo bay area of a Chinook. The typical early-model Cargo/Troop Carrying Hummer weighed in at about 5,200lb and could carry a payload of 2,500lb of personnel, weapons and cargo. *US Army*

incorporating new standards of reliability in a combat vehicle. It scored high on the RAM-D tests, and during Initial Production Tests proved to be nearly twice as durable as the U.S. Army had required.

Another great advantage it has over other vehicles is its unique multipurpose platform. It has dozens of different configurations most off which share a common chassis and drivetrain. It also means a much more simplified supply, mainte-

nance, and logistics system: essentially one set of common parts for numerous configurations, and that means lower life cycle costs.

High ground clearance is a prerequisite for superior mobility. The Hummer has a full 16in, a remarkable engineering feat considering that it stands only 69in high. High ground clearance, full-time four-wheel drive, independent suspension, steep approach and departure angles, sixty percent grade capability on most models and 60in

The typical Hummer is about 6ft tall, 15ft long and 7ft wide. This wide stance provides a very stable, road hugging vehicle that is almost impossible to roll over on even the steepest inclines. By contrast, the older M151 Jeep was 5ft 9in tall, about 12ft long, and 4ft 4in wide. While this small size made

the M151 Jeep very nimble in confined spaces, it also made the vehicle somewhat unstable and prone to rolling over. Hiding at the edge of a tree line, this camouflaged US Army Hummer blends in very well with the background.

water-fording capability make the Hummer an exceptional off-road vehicle.

A curb weight of approximately 5,100lbs in early models, and a V-8 diesel engine, with a 25gal fuel tank, gave the Hummer impressive speed, agility, and range. It can accelerate from 0-30mph in seven seconds, and has a range of up to 350 miles.

It is lean, light, and compact, and can move out quickly in strategic airlift and tactical heliborne operations. Three Hummers can be deployed in the C-130 transport, six in the C-141B ,and fifteen in the C-5A. In tactical operations, two Hummers can be carried by the CH-47 helicopter, while one can be slung from the UH-60A and CH-53 helicopters. All models except the Maxi-Ambulance can be air-dropped by LAPES.

The performance potential of the Hummer is unlimited, due mostly to the versatility of its multi-purpose platform and its ability to accommodate a wide range of weapons systems.

Pictured during a field training exercise, conducted at the US Army's National Training Center, is a mortar squad of the famous 82nd Airborne Division. The soldiers have just deployed their 120mm mortar and are adjusting the legs of the weapon prior to a firing mission. Because of its outstanding cross-country mobility, American soldiers have started to use the Hummer in a variety of roles never envisioned by its builders. *Greg Stewart*

CHAPTER 2

Military Hummers

When first built for US military service, the Hummer was configured through the use of a common chassis with common components and different add-on kits to become six different vehicle types: the Cargo-Troop Carrier; the Armament Carrier; the TOW Missile Carrier; the Ambulance Carrier; the Shelter Carrier, and the Prime Mover.

Based upon these six types, more than twenty subtypes were developed, many of which differed from one another only in minor details. For example, there were seven different subtypes of the Cargo/Troop Carrier and eight different subtypes of the Armament Carrier available at one time. In response to US military needs, AM General has updated and added new models to its production line while discontinuing others.

The most numerous Hummer variant in US military service has always been the M998 Cargo/Troop Carrier pictured here. In fact, the M998 designation represents the entire Hummer family of US military vehicles. Most all of the other versions of the US military Hummers are based on this one vehicle type. Over the years, improvements to this basic M998 vehicle have resulted in an M998A1 and M998A2 series of Hummer vehicles now produced by AM General and fielded by US military forces around the world. _AM General_

AM General and the US military refer to the entire Hummer fleet as either the M998, M998A1, or M998A2 model, without regard to particular model designations.

Heavy Hummer Variant

Because of increasing weight-carrying demands by US military forces in 1991, AM General began modifying its existing Hummer chassis with an upgraded suspension/drivetrain to increase the gross vehicle weight to 10,000lb and the payload to 4,400lb thus resulting in the M1097 Heavy Hummer Variant (HHV). This was accomplished with minimum changes to the chassis, and no changes to the engine.

The M1097 Heavy Hummer Variant (HHV) was type classified Standard in May 1992 and entered production for the US Army in September 1992.

The HHV Variant could accommodate a larger number of communication shelters, weapon systems, logistics support systems, and boasted increased ballistic protection and towing capabilities.

One of the shelters fitted to the HHV was the Army's Standardized Integrated Command Post System (SICPS) shelter. The SICPS is a family of command post facilities developed to house the Army Tactical Command and Control System. Each shelter is equipped with a five-kilowatt power unit, an air conditioner unit, a collective chemical-biological protection system, equipment racks, and power and signal import-export panels, plus intercom and operator seats.

The A1 Series Hummer

In early 1994, AM General began production of the M998A1 series of Hummers. All A1 models of the US military Hummer fleet incorporated the M1097 Heavy Hummer Variant (HHV) chassis components, plus new front seats, an improved parking brake lever with safety release, a metal hood grille, an improved slave receptacle, a solid state glow plug controller, modified rifle mounts, and upgraded rear half shafts. The use of these common chassis components enhanced standardization across all models, thus leading to improvements in logistical support, ease of training, and increased fleet durability.

Depending on its mission and weather conditions the US military Hummer can be open-or closed-topped and fitted with a removable roll bar. Pictured at the National Training Center (NTC), located in the desert region of Southern California, this Hummer crew from the 3rd Armored Cavalry Regiment is taking a break in a training exercise. Due to the extreme desert heat, this four-door Hummer has been stripped of all its doors and its rooftop, but not the roll bar. *Greg Stewart*

The M1037 and M1042 Shelter Carriers were replaced by the M1097A1 Cargo/Troop Carrier, even though large numbers of the M1037 and M1042 will be in the Army inventory for many years to come. The Gross Vehicle Weight (GVW) rating for all A1 models of the military Hummer, except for the M1097, were increased by approximately 180lb; vehicle payloads and towed load capacities remained the same.

The A2 Series Hummer

Even as AM General began building the new M998A1 series in 1994, they decided to go one step further and came up with a Hummer that was even better: the M998A2. This series started coming off production line in 1995. Using the M1097A1 HHV as a baseline, the new series incorporated a 6.5 liter naturally aspirated diesel engine generating 160hp, electronically controlled four-speed automatic transmission, and a redesigned emissions system which met all of the 1995 US Government standards.

Other enhancements to the M998A2 series included increased cargo bed tie down capacity, an improved heater system, new rear seats similar to the A1 series front seats, self-canceling turn

For cold and wet weather conditions, the US military Hummer comes with a wide variety of soft-top plastic and fabric enclosures. This US Army Hummer is fitted out with a four-seater plastic top which extends all the way over the rear cargo bay. Depending on the crew's needs the rear cargo space can be covered or uncovered.

signals, an improved steering wheel and column, LED side marker lights, and improved transportability tie down provisions. All vehicles were also built to be "CTI ready", that is, ready to accept a Central Tire Inflation System as a field installed item. Since that time, all US military Hummers are delivered CTI-ready.

Up-Armored Hummers

AM General took advantage of the HHV chassis to develop an armor protection system for its weapon carriers. This system consists of ballistic panels that are applied to the various HHV armament and TOW Missile Carriers to defeat both 7.62mm and 5.56mm ball ammo.

The additional ballistic materials are selectively applied to both the exterior and interior of the vehicle. Maximum protection from ground attack is provided to the crew and vital automotive components. Optimum visibility and protection are provided with 1.6in nonspalling ballistic glazing material. Roof, crew floor, and weapon

All military Hummers have the provision for having four doors. For some variants of the Hummer in which the two rear doors are not needed, aluminum or simple wood fillets are used to close off the door openings. The fabric tops for military Hummers come in high or low-profile versions and are supported by metal lateral bows.

Belonging to the 1st Cavalry Division, this Hummer has been configured as a troop carrier. In this configuration the vehicle can carry a two-person crew and eight passengers on bench seats in the rear of the vehicle. Taking part in a large training exercise, the crew of this Hummer removed the glass from the vehicle's front windshield in order to cut down on reflection, which might give away their position at sunrise or sunset. *Greg Stewart*

station armor protect against weapons as powerful as 7.62mm machine gun ball ammunition.

The up-armored HHV successfully completed AM General's full-scale live firing tests and independent durability and performance testing in 1992.

A small number of the HHVs were then sold to an unnamed foreign country. Due to budget constraints, the US military was not interested in buying any of the up-armored HHVs. That changed, however, later in 1992 when US troops were sent to Somalia as part of a United Nations peace-keeping force. The US Army Military Police quickly found that their Hummers (Armament Carriers with the basic armor kit) were little match for an enemy equipped with AK47s and hand-held rocket-propelled grenade launchers (RPGs). Trapped in urban settings, escorting slow-moving truck convoys, the Hummer's outstanding mobility offered little protection against the ambushes and hit and run tactics of the Somali militiamen.

As a stop-gap measure to help even the odds, the US Army quickly ordered about fifty up-armored HHVs for its military police units on duty

Standard practice for crews of US military Hummers who are not interested in removing their vehicle's window glass every time they travel into the field, is to raise the front hood of the vehicles as soon as it is parked. This is the easiest and fastest way to cut down on any possible window reflection. This Hummer was part of the now disbanded 7th Light Infantry Division based at Fort Ord, California.

in Somalia. These vehicles were designated XM1109.

The XM1109 provided its crew compartment, but not the engine compartment or rear cargo bay, with a much higher level of protection as compared to earlier Hummers. Unlike the US Army's original fleet of armament carrier Hummers, which offered protection only from bullet fragments, the XM1109 provided 360 degree protection for its crew from 7.62mm NATO armor piercing rounds and from 155mm artillery airburst fragments. Underbody protection on the XM1109 was designed to protect its crew from 4lb antiper-

sonnel mine or a 12lb antitank mine. That doesn't mean the vehicle itself would be operational after running over such mines, but in most cases the crew would survive.

AM General does not manufacture the armored components that make up the various Up-Armored Hummers. Instead, they rely on the O'Gara-Hess & Eisenhardt Armoring Company of Fairfield, Ohio.

Founded in 1876, this company has long specialized in modifying existing civilian vehicles to become armored vehicles for the protection of heads of state and corporate executives from

The Hummer Armament Carrier in US Army service is fitted with only the barest minimum of armor protection. The aluminum and fiberglass doors on the vehicle offer protection against bullet fragments only. The distinctive X-shaped stamping on the doors increases rigidity. The vehicle pictured is an US Army Armament Carrier taking part in "Operation Just Cause," the December 1989 invasion of Panama by US military forces. *US Army*

around the world. They have supplied armored vehicles for every United States President from Harry Truman to present.

The XM1109 Hummer configuration turned out to be only an interim project designed to answer a specific US Army need at that time.

Expanded Capacity Vehicle

To fulfill the US Army's requirement for a Hummer with armor protection levels equal to the Up-Armored XM1109 Hummer and with no loss in cargo-carrying ability, AM General and O'Gara, Hess and Eisenhardt began delivery of a new Up-Armored Hummer based on AM General's Expanded Capacity Vehicle (ECV) in 1995.

The ECV was developed by AM General under US Government contract to further enhance the Hummer family of vehicles. The ECV has a payload capability of 5,300lb compared to the 4,400lb payload of an normal M1097A2 Cargo/

Like all other variants of the Hummer in US military service, the Armament Carrier has been improved over the years. The original M1025 (and the winch-equipped M1026) was updated to the A1 standard. With the introduction of the A2 standard, only the M1025A2 survived into production. The M1025A2 was also modified to mount a TOW Missile Launcher system. Pictured is a M966 US Army Armament Carrier mounting a TOW running at high speed. *Greg Stewart*

Due to increasing weight-carrying demands made by the US military, AM General developed a new version of the Hummer in 1991 known as the M1097 Heavy Hummer Variant (HHV). This improved Hummer featured an upgraded suspension and drivetrain but still used the original 150hp GM V8 6.2 Liter diesel fuel injected engine. This vehicle had a greater payload which allowed it to carry a greater number of communication shelters or weapon systems. Pictured is a HHV mounting a US Army communication shelter. *AM General*

Troop/Shelter Carrier Hummer. The curb weight increased from 5,900lb to 6,200lb.

To retain the Hummer's outstanding mobility despite its rise in weight, it was fitted with a 6.5L turbo diesel engine generating 190hp.

The ECV also utilized a great many of the improved components developed for AM General's Cab-Over Hummer Variant (COHHV) cargo truck. These components include modified differentials, improved halfshafts, new exhaust system, improved brakes, improved cooling system, improved suspension, modified steering system, upgraded wheels and a reinforced frame.

Beginning in 1995, the US Military's Up-Armored ECVs came equipped with AM General's Central Tire Inflation System and an Air Conditioning unit. Both these features had been available on civilian Hummers since 1992.

The US Army has designated the Up-Armored ECV as the M1113. Two different ver-

In early 1994, AM General began to base the entire Hummer family on the HHV chassis. While still equipped with the original Hummer diesel engine, this vehicle incorporated a number of component improvements. To reflect the many changes made to the US military Hummer fleet, this new model was designated as the M998A1. Pictured at the National Training Center is a Shelter Carrier version, M1037. *Greg Stewart*.

sions of the M1113 in Army service are the M1114 Armament Carrier and the M1115 TOW Missile Carrier. These vehicles are not designed to replace the Army's existing fleet of Hummer armament carriers or TOW missile carriers, but rather to be used in certain units for scouting applications.

US Air Force Security Police units have also been issued a variant of the Army's M1113. In Air Force use, the vehicle is designated as the M1116.

Cargo-Troop Carrier

One of the most common Hummer variants in US military service is the M998 Cargo/Troop Carrier. Fitted with a winch, the basic M998 vehicle is known as the M1038.

Beginning in 1994, the M998 variants were upgraded to an A1 standard, which incorporated a number of component enhancements.

In 1995, AM General began production of yet another upgraded Hummer standard which became known as the A2, and this resulted in some designation changes to the US military's fleet of Hummers. The upgraded A2 Hummers were designed to supplement (not replace) the existing fleet of M998 Cargo/Troop Carriers and M1037 Shelter Carriers.

Prior to the fielding of the new A2 standard Hummers, the M1037 Hummer Shelter Carrier fitted with a winch was designated as the M1042. With the introduction of the A2 there is no longer a separate designation for vehicles fitted with a winch. This was done for two reasons. Firstly, to help simplify the Army's nomenclature and secondly, because the Army now sees the winch as an optional component and not as a standard part of the vehicle: it can be fitted or removed from their Hummers based on mission needs.

Externally there is almost nothing to distinguish the newer A2 models from the older models or the A1 production models. All Hummers have

the provision for four doors. For some variants, aluminum or simple wood fillets are used to close off these doors.

Late in 1994, AM General decided to upgrade the A1 Hummer by incorporating a new more powerful GM V8 6.5 liter naturally aspirated diesel engine, which generated 160hp. As a result of this engine change, the new Hummer was designated as the M998A2. There were also a number of other minor improvements made to the A2 model vehicles. As before, the external modifications on most Hummers are so slight that it is almost impossible to tell the difference between the first production vehicle and the newest versions. *AM General*

Under a US Army contract, AM General developed a Hummer called the Expanded Capacity Vehicle (ECV). It is based on a newly developed Hummer chassis with greater weight-carrying ability and equipped with a 6.5 liter Turbo diesel engine generating 190hp. The first variant of this new Hummer model was the M1113 Up-Armored Hummer, which was designed to protect its crew compartment from a wide variety of weapon threats. The first production models were delivered to the US Army in 1995. *O'Gara Hess & Eisenhardt*

Depending on its mission and weather conditions, the older model M998/M998A1 Hummer as well as the newer A2 model can be open- or closed-topped and be fitted with a removable roll bar. The front windshield on all Hummers cannot normally be folded down on the front hood of the vehicle as was possible with the WW2 era and postwar era Jeeps.

It became apparent shortly after the first Hummers were deployed in training exercises by the US Army that the reflections from the fixed front-mountedwindshields could be seen for miles

AM General's Up-Armored M1097A1/A2 Hummer has been offered to both US military forces and a number of allies. Like the entire Hummer series, the M1097A1/A2 can be configured in a number of different ways. The Hummer pictured is mounting a 40mm grenade launcher in an armored one-man turret. This vehicle also features a square-back rear cargo covering. The square back rear cargo covering or the slanted rear cargo door found on the M1097A1/A2 can be armored or unarmored. *AM General*

during sunrise and sunset. In combat this could be a deadly giveaway if an enemy observer was looking for US military positions. To prevent this from being a problem in combat, all US military Hummers in the field must raise their front hoods when parked for any length of time or cover their fixed front windshields with some type camouflage, or even a simple blanket. To solve this problem, many American soldiers have either completely removed the windshield from the soft-top versions of the Hummer or have simply removed all the glass from the windows in the hard-top versions.

The older M998/M998A1 model Hummer and the newer A2 model Hummer are normally fitted with a number of different plastic tops. The

The Expanded Capacity Vehicle (ECV) is an enhancement of the growing Hummer family. Besides a bigger engine and a four-speed automatic transmission, the vehicle uses a large number of components from AM General's medium capacity cargo truck known as the Cab-Over-Hummer. This

AM General-designed cargo truck comes in three different configurations: a flatbed dropside cargo carrier as pictured, a low-bed shelter carrier, and a simple cab and chassis which a customer equips as necessary. *AM General* tops come in either high- or low-profile versions and are supported by metal lateral bows.

As a troop carrier, the M998/M998A1 model and the new A2 model vehicle can carry a two person crew and eight seated passengers on wooden bench seats. As a cargo and troop carrier, the M998/M998A1 or the A2 model can be fitted with a plastic top covering four seats and a small cargo space in the rear which can be either covered or uncovered.

The older M998/M998A1 Hummer fleet or the newer A2 Hummer vehicles can also be fitted with a weapon-station mount for a number of weapons systems including a 40mm grenade launcher, or .50 caliber machine gun. Other weapons systems that can be fitted on the M1097A2 include a TOW missile launcher, a 30mm automatic cannon, and even a .50 caliber GAU-19/A three barrel Gatling gun.

Other armies supplied with the older-model M998/M998A1 Hummers have taken to mounting a wide variety of American and foreign-built weapons systems ranging from large antiaircraft machine guns to 106mm recoilless rifles on their

This US Army M997A1 Maxi-Ambulance is not bullet-proof, but does offer protection from shell and bullet fragments. It does provide both air conditioning and heat. *AM General*

vehicles. In most cases this has meant the removal of the fixed front windshield found on all Hummers troop carriers.

Armament Carrier

Another common Hummer variant is the M1025 Armament Carrier. With a winch it is known as the M1026. In 1994, AM General began to produce an M1025A1 and M1026A1 Armament Carrier. In 1995, AM General began production of the newest version of the armament carrier, known as the M1025A2.

Both the older and newer versions of the Armament Carrier are configured for transportation of appropriate weapons with their supporting crews and equipment. The weapon-station design emphasizes simplicity and flexibility of operation as well as accessibility of components for easy maintenance. The armament mounting kit features a thirty-two-inch weapon ring with a

The M1069 Hummer Prime Mover is designed to tow the Army's 105mm M119 Light Artillery Howitzer, which is clearly seen in this picture. To help carry the large camouflage net that helps to hide the howitzer in the field, the Prime Mover is equipped with a large rack over the driver's compartment. *Greg Stewart*

pintle mount and a quick-release cradle. Mounted weapons have a 360 degree circle of fire. The mounting kit can accommodate the 40mm automatic grenade launcher, the M2 .50cal machine gun, the M60 7.62mm machine gun, or the new M240 7.62mm machine gun.

TOW Missile Carrier

Originally, the M966 TOW Missile Carrier (fitted with a winch it was known as the M1036) was designed as a combat vehicle for the transportation of US Army and Marine Corps antitank missile teams.

The US Army has decided combine two Hummer variants (three model numbers) into a single chassis model. These are the newer M1025A2 Armament Carrier and the older generation M996 and M1036 TOW Missile Carriers. The US Marine Corps decided to keep the two vehicle models separate. One model, known as the M1043A2, will continue to carry only machine guns or the 40mm grenade launcher while another model, known as the M1045A2, will be use only as a TOW Missile Carrier.

The US Army has recently taken advantage of the greater weight-carrying payload of the M1025A2 series Hummers to mount the TOW Missile system. The US Army has allowed AM General to discontinue the production of the M996/M1036 Tow Missile Carrier. This decision does not mean the older generation of armament carriers will disappear from the US Army fleet. It only means that there will be a number of improved M1025A2 Hummers carrying the TOW Missile System in the Army's inventory.

The TOW missile has been the main antitank weapon used by the US Army and US Marine Corps since the 1970s. Work first began on the missile in 1965.

With a range of almost three miles on newer models, the TOW missile carries a high-explosive, armor-piercing-shaped-charge warhead that pro-

duces enough heat to burn through the thickest armor when it hits an enemy tank.

The US Army and US Marine Corps Hummers fitted with the TOW Missile system can carry the entire TOW crew with the complete weapon system and associated equipment. Stowage in the cargo compartment of the vehicle is designed to facilitate rapid TOW mounting and reloading. All TOW carriers have a two-way cargoloader door for up-loading the missiles and reloading the TOW launcher itself. The TOW crew can rapidly dismount the system for ground use, if needed. There are provisions for carrying six reload missiles in the various TOW missile carrying Hummers.

It's fairly common to see many Armament Carriers and TOW Missile Carrier versions of the Hummer without any window glass at all. Besides cutting down on possible reflections from the window glass at sunrise or sunset, US Army scouts have learned during training and real combat that with the windows up and the heater running in a Hummer, hearing is very limited. It has been observed that if one is able to hear the enemy before he hears you, half the battle is won.

According to confirmed reports, TOW-equipped Hummers destroyed a number of Iraqi tanks during Operation Desert Storm.

The doors on the hard-top ambulances, and on the various weapon-carrying variants of the Hummer military family of vehicles are made of fiberglass reinforced with a bulletproof-vest type material called E-Glass which bears a distinctive X-shaped stamping on the panel to increase rigidity. The aluminum and fiberglass components on the Hummer provide a certain degree of armor protection from fragments, but are not bullet-proof like an M1 tank.

The aluminum and fiberglass doors on weapon-carrying Hummer variants have a polycarbonate bullet-resistant window that slides up and down on metal tracks. The front windshield is also bullet-resistant to a certain extent, but not bullet-proof.

The US Marine Corps weapon-carrying Hummer variants have been equipped with an additional "supplemental armor kit" consisting of thin, flat steel plates affixed to the doors and other surfaces. This armor kit provides more protection from fragments, but roughly the same protection against bullets.

The supplemental armor kit and special deep water fording kits often fitted to US Marine Corps Hummers are the best way to distinguish them from the US Army Hummers.

The deep water fording kit consists of an exhaust pipe extension that runs all the way to the top of the rear of the vehicle on the driver's side. An extended air intake pipe is located at the rear of the engine hood on the passenger's side. With the deep water fording kit, the Hummer can cross 60in of water; without it, only 30in.

Both Army and Marine Corps weapon-carrying Hummer variants have hood grills with louvers which are backed up by baffles to prevent bullets or shell fragments from damaging the vehicles' radiators.

In the US Army, the weapon-carrying Hummers play an essential role in current mounted-warfare doctrine. The Hummer equipped scout provides his battlefield commander with the most critical information: combat intelligence. To accomplish this mission, the scout needs a high mobility, stealthy vehicle which can fight it out with the enemy when needed, take a punch, and be able to transmit vital information to headquarters. The Hummer does that and more. According to many American soldiers, "The Hummer is one of the best investments the US Army has made in years. The vehicle requires little maintenance, is quick, yet relatively quiet, is very maneuverable on all types of terrain, and has a range of almost 300 miles on a single tank of fuel."

To enhance the Hummer's role as the eyes and ears of the modern US Army, such items as a new advanced pintle weapons mount for weapon-carrying Hummers and a new thermal sight known as the PAS13 are to be fitted in the near future to the Army's scout Hummers. Other items that could be fitted to future Hummer scout vehicles may include VHF (Single Channel Group

The strangest Hummer variant yet to be seen in US Army service resides at the Army's National Training Center, located in the desert region of Southern California. Based on a standard Hummer Armament Carrier, the US Army modified two dozen of these vehicles into vague copies of the Soviet Army BRDM2 armored cars. Fitted out with fiberglass bodywork to simulate the real thing, they have been very successful as training aids.

and Airborne Radio Subsystem, or SINCGARS) radios and mounts and a Global Positioning System and mounting provisions.

Ambulance Carrier

The Hummer ambulance family used to include three variants: the M1035 Soft-Top and the hardtop M996 Mini and M997 Maxi Ambulances. Each ambulance variant offered the outstanding off-road capability for which the Hummer has always been known.

Beginning in 1994, AM General discontinued production of the M996 Mini Ambulance. Those M996 Mini Ambulances already in the US military inventory will remain in service. Both the Soft-Top and Maxi-Ambulances are now being built for the A2 series of Hummers. The Soft-Top Ambulance is being designated as the M1035A2 and the Maxi-Ambulance as the M997A2.

The Soft-top Ambulance is a basic Hummer fitted with a low-profile soft-top enclosure equipped to carry two litter patients, three ambu-

Shown at the US Army's National Training Center is the Avenger antiaircraft system. The Avenger consists of a four-tube Stinger antiaircraft missile launcher mounted on a pedestal on each side of an operator's station, which in turn is mounted on an Hummer. A .50 caliber machine gun can be mounted beneath the right side Stinger launcher for close-up defensive duties. *Greg Stewart*

latory patients, and a driver. It transports patients quickly from field to hospital. Only the Marine Corps uses this variant.

The Maxi Ambulances mounts a special shelter on the Hummer platform and is equipped to provide comprehensive medical care to wounded soldiers.

Storage areas and compartments are provided on the Maxi Ambulance. A 200 amp alternator and fragmentation protection are standard features on this vehicle. An integral environment control unit in the Maxi Ambulance provides air conditioning or heating for comfortable mobile conditions.

Shelter Carrier

The now discontinued M1037 Shelter Carrier configuration (existing models will remain in service for many years to come) is equipped with a heavy-duty suspension system, a heavy-duty airlift bumper, and built-in brackets to secure the shelter to the Hummer chassis. With a winch the vehicle was known as the M1042.

The shelter carrier mounted on the mobile Hummer vehicle normally carries communications gear such as radios, battlefield computers, and a variety of other electronic equipment which requires greater protection from the elements than provided by the simple plastic top as fitted to the M998/M1038 Hummer cargo/troop carrier.

Prime Mover

The Hummer is the designated prime mover for the US Army's 105mm light artillery howitzers. It provides Army and Marine Corps field artillery units with the ability to move these weapons over all but the roughest terrains.

With the introduction of the new M119 Light Artillery Howitzer, the US Army began to use a specially modified Hummer originally designated as the M1069. This variant is still in service and can be spotted by the large rack above the dri-ver's compartment which is designed to carry a large camouflage net for the 105mm gun when deployed in the field.

The M119 is an American-made derivative of the British-built L119 Light Gun. It is a lightweight, 105mm, towed howitzer which improves fire support for the Army's airborne, air assault and light infantry divisions, and separate brigades. It will replace all older generation M102 howitzers in the active force. It can fire all conventional 105mm ammunition currently in the Army inventory and the new high-explosive rocket-assisted ammunition currently in production.

Because of its light weight and low profile, the M1069 Hummer and M119 are transportable in the C-130 and the C-41B aircraft and by the CH-47 and CH-53 helicopters. Fewer missions are required to lift a battalion of Hummers and M119 howitzers than would be required to deploy the same size unit equipped with larger prime movers.

Soviet-Style Variant

The strangest Hummer variants in service with the US Army are located at Fort Irwin in southern California, home of the National Training Center (NTC). Here, in an area of almost 1,000 square miles of sun-baked terrain, the Army constructed the world's most sophisticated and realistic simulated battlefield.

To provide worthy, realistic opposition for the troops coming to the NTC for training, the Army created a unit designated as the Opposing Force (OPFOR). The members of the OPFOR represent major elements of a Soviet Army motorized regiment. Since it is not practical to use large numbers of real Soviet-built equipment in training, the Army modified a number of American vehicles to become vague copies of their Soviet Army counterparts.

Since the Soviet Army has always employed a large number of wheeled scout cars, the US Army uses a small number of Hummer M998 Cargo-Troop Carriers fitted out with fiberglass body-work to replicate or simulate Soviet BRDM-2 scout cars. The modified Hummers employed by the OPFOR at the NTC have accurately portrayed their Soviet counterparts in hundreds of NTC training exercises.

Stinger Missile Carrier

The Stinger antiaircraft missile as used by the US Army is a shoulder-launched system. The two-person Stinger teams use a M998 or newer M998A1/A2 Cargo/Troop Carrier for transport.

Each of these vehicles is equipped with two radios and a basic missile load of eight Stingers carried in four-round racks that fit in the rear cargo bay of the Hummer.

The Stinger is a shoulder-fired, infrared homing missile antiaircraft system. The missile homes in on the heat emitted by either jet- or propeller-driven aircraft and helicopters. A Stinger crew visually acquires its target and electronically interrogates it to help determine if it is a friend. The missile notifies the gunner when it has a "lock" on the target. After the trigger is pulled, the

The modern military Hummer is huge compared to the WW2 era Jeep. But next to this thirty ton US Army M2A3 Bradley Fighting Vehicle, the Hummer doesn't seem so large. In today's modern Army, the Bradley and Hummer share the battalion level scouting duties. While the Bradley has a much higher survival rate due to its armor protection and 25mm cannon, the Hummer is much faster, quieter, not as fuel hungry, and is much easier to hide on a battlefield. *Greg Stewart*

Stinger is ejected from the tube by a small launcher motor. Once the missile has traveled a safe distance from the gunner, its main engine ignites and propels it to the target. The Stinger is stored in a sealed tube, requires no maintenance in the field, and is designed to withstand the rigors of the battlefield.

The Avenger

A very impressive Hummer variant in service with the US Army is the Avenger. The Avenger system consists of eight ready-to-fire Stinger missiles and a .50 caliber machine gun integrated with sensors and target acquisition devices.

The integrated Avenger system provides all the necessary functions to detect, acquire, track, and identify friendly or enemy aircraft with either the missile or the machine gun during the day or night and in adverse weather conditions. Its standard vehicle-mounted launchers interface and can function with all the various models of the Stinger that have been produced.

The Avenger system is mounted on the older generation Hummer Shelter Carrier, model

Pictured in the middle of the vast, barren terrain that makes up the US Army's National Training Center (NTC) is a US Army M966 Mini Ambulance Carrier, which belongs to the now disbanded 7th Light Infantry Division. The vehicle as shown is not being used as an ambulance but as a command and control vehicle. In the background is an M998 Cargo/Troop Carrier used by the umpires based at the NTC. *Greg Stewart*

M1037. Future production models may be mounted on the M1097A2 Cargo/Troop/Shelter Carrier chassis.

The vehicle has a two-person crew that can fire its missiles on the move or operate the missile system from a distance with a remote control device. Its mission is to counter hostile, low-flying, high-speed, fixed-wing aircraft and helicopters attacking US Army formations.

The builder of the Avenger system is the Boeing Aerospace Company. The Avenger went into full-scale production in April 1990.

Besides the Hummers designed and built for the US military, AM General has designed a number of special kits to expand the mission capability and flexibility of its Hummer chassis. The vehicle pictured combines a number of Up-Armored components as well as a 30mm cannon. AM General sees this type of vehicle as a perfect choice for Desert Operations, Reconnaissance, Security, and Special Operation missions. *AM General*

CHAPTER 3

Civilian Hummers

The wide spread television exposure that the US military's fleet of Hummers received during Operation Desert Shield and Operation Desert Storm convinced many Americans that the Hummer was something they had to have. The most well-known individual wanting a Hummer was actor Arnold Schwarzenegger, who contacted AM General directly and managed to talk the company into selling him a custom-built model. With the strong urging of Schwarzenegger and hundreds of other asking to buy civilian versions of the Hummer, AM General announced to the press in late June 1991 that it would start building a civilian version of the battle-tested Hummer. The first civilian Hummer rolled off the AM General production line in late 1992.

Of the many special options available for the civilian Hummer owner, the most interesting is

Relentlessly tested, combat proven, built to the most demanding military specifications, the Hummer is the world's most serious 4x4 off-road vehicle. With an unmatched 16in of ground clearance, wide track stability of 72in, powerful wheel-end torque, four-wheel independent suspension, and full-time 4x4 drive, the Hummer sets a new standard for civilian off-road vehicles. *AM General*

the Central Tire Inflation System, or CTI. No other 4x4 vehicle in the civilian market has this feature. CTI allows the driver to change tire pressure on-the-move to suit terrain conditions. With the CTI system, the air passes through the geared hub assembly. Air hoses lead from an on-board compressor to the inside center of each geared hub. The spindle then acts as the air passageway through the hub. A connecting hose at the outside center of the spindle routes the air to the tire.

The CTI system is easily operated using two main controls: the inflate/deflate switch and the tire selector valve, which work as a team. The driver simply turns the tire selector valve to the desired setting — front tires, rear tires, or both front and rear — and then chooses inflate or deflate to reach the desired tire pressure. An air pressure gauge located on the dash enables the operator to continuously monitor tire pressure.

CTI offers two main advantages: added traction and a smoother ride. When operating on sand, mud, or any kind of soft soil, lowering tire pressure results in a larger "footprint" on the ground, increasing traction for better mobility. At the same time, lowering the tire pressure makes the tires softer, enhancing the ride. This is a benefit even when added mobility isn't needed, but the terrain is very rugged. Softer tires result in less driver fatigue, less passenger fatigue, and actually contributes to the durability of the chassis by minimizing shock and vibration.

For even better off-road traction and handling, 37x12.5 inch Goodyear Wrangler tires are available. These larger tires are mounted on a two-piece take-apart wheel with an intricate

AM General designed the Hummer to go almost anywhere you can think of. Aided by a seventy-two degree approach angle, a fully loaded Hummer will climb and descend a vertical slope of up to sixty percent and climb a 22in vertical step. It will also traverse a forty percent side slope. *AM General*

bead-lock and run-flat assembly that allows the Hummer to be driven with one or more of its tires completely flat for up to thirty miles on soft terrain. A rear-mounted swingaway spare tire carrier and spare tire are available.

To further protect the major driveline components, a driveline protection package is available with skid plates and mounted steel tubes. Guard and rocker panel protection are also available.

The Hummer can also be equipped with a trailer towing package which includes a receiver hitch assembly allowing the Hummer to tow as much as 8,000lb. As standard equipment, each civilian Hummer has an 124 amp alternator to meet additional electrical requirements when trailering.

Also available is an electrically-powered Warn winch with a 12,000lb capacity. This

The macho-looking Hummer will never win any contests for beauty. Certainly nobody will ever call it cute. AM General designed the Hummer as a tough, serious, and reliable 4x4 vehicle that could go places that no other manufacturer's 4x4 could ever dream of. The Hummer's design was based on rigorous military standards that demanded it be able to operate anywhere in the world under the most adverse conditions with a minimum of maintenance. Shown are two civilian Hummers doing a little rock climbing. *AM General*

While many 4x4 off-road vehicle buffs (who have never driven a Hummer) may decry the Hummer's width and overall size as a problem during off-roading in close quarters. Few of them realize that the Hummer doesn't have to go around most terrain obstacles, it goes right over them. Pictured is a winch-equipped Hummer coming straight up a hill. *AM General*

rugged winch is more than capable of retrieving the Hummer or another vehicle.

Anyone who has driven a Hummer knows how rugged it is. But they're also discovering just how comfortable it is. Optional interior features include air conditioning, deluxe interior package with upgraded trim, and premium sound system (front and rear), lighting package with courtesy lights, rear cargo area light, and sliding rear window.

AM General offers a number of different body styles including softtops and hardtops.

The Hummer is built to last. And, it's built for safety, meeting or exceeding all Federal Motor Vehicle Standards for Class III trucks. Safety features on civilian Hummers include a collapsible steering column, padded dashboard, steel roof, and steel doors with side impact beams and a three-point seat belt system. *AM General*

In terms of safety, the Hummer meets or exceeds all Federal Motor Vehicle Safety Standards for Class III trucks. Specific safety features include a collapsible steering column, padded dashboard, steel doors with side-impact beams, and a three-point seat-belt system.

The Hummer is also built to last, meeting the same tough quality specifications as its military counterparts built in the same assembly plant which earned the U.S. Army's highest honor for quality manufacturing. AM General backs the Hummer's quality with a 36-month/36,000 mile bumper-to-bumper warranty.

The Hummer's automotive technology is pretty straight forward. As a result, the Hummer is very easy to maintain, much like a passenger car,

Compared to any other 4x4 vehicle on the civilian market today, the Hummer is probably the most technologically advanced. In fact, because of its straight forward engineering, the Hummer is maintained very much like a passenger car. Changing the oil every 3,000 miles and cleaning or replacing the air filter every so often is all the Hummer ordinarily requires. *AM General*

checking the engine oil and filter, changing it about every 3,000 miles, cleaning or replacing the air filter periodically. Standard automotive maintenance is all the Hummer requires.

The 1994 civilian Hummer featured changes to the powertrain, the electrical system, the heating and cooling system, the body and interior, and the chassis, yet still retains the Hummer's unique character and performance capabilities.

One of the big changes for the 1994 civilian Hummer was an entirely new powertrain, standard on all models, comprised of a new engine

To help prove how durable and dependable Hummers can be, AM General developed two modified civilian vehicles that were entered into the grueling fifty-six-day London to Peking Motoring Challenge in 1990. During this event, the two Hummers traveled over 9,000 miles across nine countries and two continents without a hitch. *AM General*

Organized by the Jules Verne Society to help commemorate the original 1907 "Great Race" from Peking to Paris, the trip itself included every type of terrain imaginable ranging from the Gobi Desert to metropolitan streets. The Hummers had been modified by AM General to have extra large fuel tanks and carry a portable satellite communications system. *AM General*

and transmission. A new General Motors Corporation 6.5 liter naturally-aspirated diesel engine provides twelve percent more horsepower and twenty percent more torque for superior performance both on the off-highway. Also new is a General Motors 4L80-E transmission. This four-speed automatic transmission provides improved torque capacity, smoother shifts, and is quieter and more fuel efficient at highway speeds.

Among the new "creature comforts" on the civilian Hummer are standard power door locks and available power windows, remote keyless

For serious off-roading—when you need to get up that hill, across that rough patch of ground, or through the snow—there's only one 4x4. The Hummer will muscle its way through 2ft of snow.

With the Hummer's lockable internal differential, it's possible to put equal power to all four wheels when added traction is needed, such as on snow-covered roads or muddy trails. *AM General*

entry system, and power mirrors. The 1994 civilian Hummer is also equipped with an electronically-controlled heating and air conditioning system that has more cooling capacity, more air flow, and improved defroster performance. Standard on four versions of the 1995 passengers models of the civilian Hummers is an auxiliary heating and air conditioning system for added comfort in even the most extreme climates.

Changes to the body and interior provide increased passenger comfort including a fully adjustable passenger seat and more rear seat leg room. The 1994 civilian Hummer also features upgraded cloth fabric seats as well as optional

In 1994, AM General began putting a new 6.5 liter naturally aspirated diesel engine in their civilian Hummer for increased performance. In 1995, AM General introduced a 5.7 liter GM V8 gasoline for buyers who wanted a choice of engine types.

Combined with the Hummer's new automatic four-speed transmission, it helped to provide better highway performance, improved fuel economy, and a quieter ride. *AM General*

Other improvements to the civilian Hummer that began with the 1994 production models included enhanced heating and air conditioning systems. Other new standard features on the 1994 models were power door locks, 124 amp alternator, improved window glass that reduces heat build up inside the vehicle, a glove box, one piece wheels, and flow-through ventilation. Options included power windows and remote keyless entry.
AM General

driver and passenger seat armrests and an available roof-mounted luggage rack.

The cargo space in the civilian Hummer passenger wagon model becomes more versatile with the ability to remove the cargo bulkhead.

A tonneau cover is now standard on both the Four Passenger Open Top and Four Passenger Hard Top models.

Other changes made to the interior of the civilian Hummer include the addition of a glove

One of the secrets of the Hummer's amazing off-road ability is due to its suspension/chassis system. The Hummer's geared hub final drive provides increased torque at each wheel end. This final gear reduction allows the drivetrain components to be mounted high inside the vehicle's chassis for maximum protection in rough terrain. *AM General*

box to all models, upgraded high quality cloth fabric seats, and the availability of driver's and passenger's seat armrests. In addition, the transfer case shift lever has been extended to facilitate shifting effort.

The exterior of the civilian Hummer sports a simplified, lighter weight rear bumper, which in no way compromises performance. The original heavy duty bumper, however, is still available as an option.

Unlike conventional 4x4s, the Hummer's axle shaft enters the geared hub a full 4in above the center of the wheel hub, which helps contribute to the Hummer's exceptional ground clearance of 16in. This means the Hummer has double the ground clearance of most other 4x4s on market today. The Hummer will clear obstacles that would turn conventional 4x4 drivelines into scrap metal. *AM General*

Each Hummer axle assembly is equipped with its own torque sensing/torque biasing differential with inboard mounted disc brakes. When one or more tires has lost traction, simply apply brake pressure, then accelerate (a technique known as "brake/throttle modulation"). This will lock the differentials and redistribute power equally to all four tires. *AM General*

One-piece wheels became standard on civilian Hummers in 1994, with the two-piece wheel available as an option. The Goodyear GS-A high speed tire is now available as an option to improve highway driving without sacrificing off-road performance. Since 1995, civilian customers have had the choice of either the 6.5 liter diesel or the 5.7 liter gasoline engine.

The Hummer is equipped with power disc brakes which provide the vehicle with exceptional stopping power, and because they are inboard mounted, they are smaller and less vulnerable to damage in rugged terrain than conventional wheel-mounted components found on the other civilian 4x4s. This unique design means true full-time four-wheel drive. *AM General*

If you run a business and need a tough, dependable work truck, the Hummer is a logical business decision. The US Government certainly thinks so. In fact, each military Hummer is expected to last a minimum of twelve years. To help convince civilian fleet administrators of the positive benefits of buying Hummers. AM General conducted a program called the Civilian Hummer Accelerated Test (CHAT) between mid-January through June 1993, in a four state vicinity of the AM General facilities in northern Indiana. *AM General*

By conducting tests such as CHAT, AM General was able to generate data to allow analytical comparisons between civilian Hummers as well as competitors' vehicles. By applying this data to formulate "Cost-per-Mile" figures, AM General can provide an accurate comparison to any other vehicle with a similar size and duty rating to interested civilian fleet administrators. *AM General*

The civilian Hummer's paint colors are as simple and functional as the Hummer itself. You can get a civilian Hummer in high gloss red, white, black, blue, tan, plum, deep green metallic, or military flat green. Pictured are four civilian Hummers in various paint schemes. *AM General*

Like its military counterparts, the civilian Hummer's family is growing in scope. With its multipurpose platform and uncompromising off-road capability, the Hummer can be configured in dozens of different ways to meet a variety of business needs. This Hummer fitted with a back-hoe. *AM General*

For any government or business organization that has to deal with a wide variety of different climate conditions, the go anywhere, anytime mobility of the Hummer and its ability to be configured with a wide variety of different attachments allows the vehicle to replace a number of more expensive specialized vehicles that are used only on a seasonal basis. Pictured is a civilian Hummer fitted out as both a snow plow and salt spreader. *AM General*

The ability of the civilian Hummer to be configured for almost any role and environment is best shown in this rare picture. Coming out of a mine entrance is a one-of-a kind Hummer which was modified to carry miners deep into the bowels of the earth. By mounting an extra large four-door equipped compartment on the rear of the basic Hummer chassis, the mining company has found a reliable and cost effective way to dispense with much more expensive specialized vehicles that used to perform such jobs. *AM General*

The Hummer's 124 amp alternator is also ideal for supporting equipment. And, the Hummer's serpentine belt easily allows the engine to be adapted with a hydraulic pump to provide full power to run special tools and equipment without excessive engine wear. Combined with the vehicle's outstanding 4x4 mobility the Hummer can provide all-year round access to off-road sites that conventional vehicles could never reach in poor weather conditions. *AM General*

The civilian Hummer can pull heavy loads, even off-road, with no problems, thanks to its powerful diesel engine, power steering, and four-speed automatic transmission (which can be shifted manually when pulling heavy loads or driving in extreme conditions for optimal performance).

Because of the Hummer's sophisticated cooling systems, engine cooling is handled by a large four core, 3in-thick radiator; there are also separate coolers for the engine, transmission, transfer case, and power steering system. *AM General*

CHAPTER *4*

Hummer Description

If there's serious off-road work to be done, either in a military role or in the civilian world, the Hummer is in a class by itself. The truth of the matter? Hummer can do things no other wheeled vehicle can do. For serious off-roading when you need to get up that hill, across that battlefield, or through that snow there's only one 4x4.

One of the first things you'll notice about the military or civilian Hummer is that it doesn't look like any other conventional 4x4 vehicle. It's wider, has greater ground clearance, yet has an overall lower silhouette. While it may not be pretty, the design is functional and based on rigorous military standards that allow the vehicle to survive in a wartime environment and results in the Hummer's tremendous performance capabilities off-road.

The overall construction of the chassis and suspension members is extremely rugged, utilizing a full-box frame with heavy duty cross members located at strategic points. All components are made of very high-grade steel for added strength and durability.

The Hummer features a four-wheel, long travel double A-arm coil spring suspension with large diameter hydraulic shock absorbers inside the coils for added protection in harsh environments. The front suspension also incorporates a large sway bar for even better handling characteristics.

An integral part of the suspension system is the wheel and tire assembly. The Hummer is equipped with large radial all-terrain tires which provide superb traction and handling characteristics both on and off-road.

The suspension system and wheel and tire assembly together allow the Hummer to provide a comfortable ride even on the roughest off-road terrain, and provide the strength to carry over two tons of cargo. One of the most unique aspects of this suspension/chassis system is the utilization of the geared hub at each corner. This geared hub final drive assembly does two things. First, the axle shaft enters the geared hub four inches above the center of the wheel hub, raising the centerline of the entire drivetrain. This contributes

According to one commercial owner of civilian Hummers: "During the winter when we experience both large snow drifts or lots of mud and the roads become impassable to conventional four-wheel drive vehicles, our Hummers consistently get us through to our work sites." *AM General*

in large part to the Hummer's exceptional ground clearance.

Second, as a two-to-one reduction hub, torque from the differential is doubled right at the wheel, making possible the use of smaller and lighter components such as axle shafts, brake components and differentials. Torque is delivered to the geared hub from a torsen along with the T-Case (in lock position) torque biasing differential with inboard mounted disk brakes, through half shafts equipped with constant velocity joints. These components are securely mounted in the chassis, between the frame rails, for maximum ground clearance and protection.

For owners of Jeep-like 4x4 vehicles, seeing a Hummer up close for the first time is usually quite a shock. The Hummer is much bigger than any Jeep. It is 180in long and 85in wide. Despite a ground clearance of 16in, the Hummer is still only 69in high, which is 2in shorter than the old Jeep. The combination of the Hummer's width and low center of gravity make it virtually impossible to roll over. *AM General*

From the ground up, the Hummer is built like no other 4x4 vehicle on earth. Supported by a boxed frame with five heavy-duty crossmembers designed to flex with the movement of the vehicle. The Hummer can easily maneuver through the most rugged terrain. The double A-frame, fully independent suspension system is supported by huge hydraulic shock absorbers which can be clearly seen in this underside picture of an Hummer chassis. *AM General*

Because they're inboard-mounted, the Hummer's four-wheel power disk brakes provide exceptional stopping power. This unique differential/ brake design also allows the Hummer to perform as a "true" full-time four-wheel drive, delivering power to all four tires even when one or more tires have lost traction. This is possible through the use of a technique known as brake/throttle modulation. When one or more tires have lost traction and are spinning, the dri-

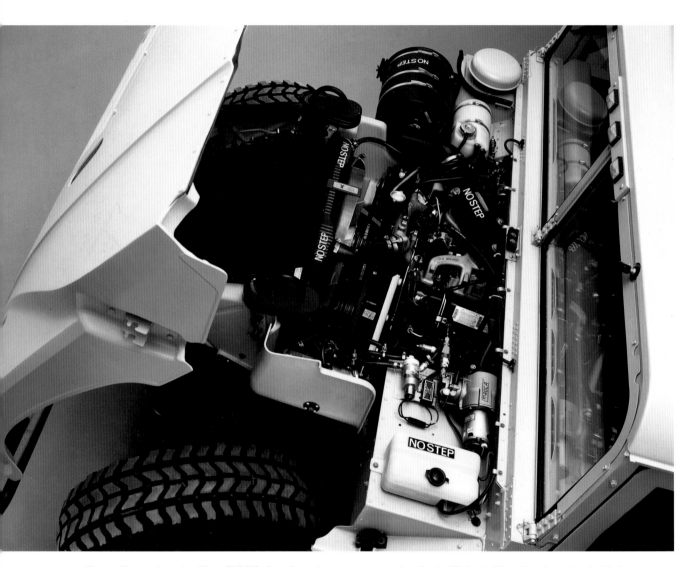

Normally equipped with a GM V8 diesel engine, newer model Hummers can develop up to 160hp and up to 290lb of foot torque at 1700rpm. Diesel engines, like the one pictured, will deliver steady power even at lower speeds. Diesel engines are also fuel efficient. The diesel engine's high compression combined with the gear ratios allows the Hummer to brake naturally while descending any slope. This translates to a lot less wear and tear on the Hummer's brake system. *AM General*

ver lightly applies brake pressure while accelerating to stop the tire spin and lock both differentials, redistributing the power equally to all four tires.

Transmitting the power to the differentials via well-protected driveshafts is the inner-cooled, two-speed New Venture Model 242 full-time four-wheel drive transfer case with a lockable internal differential. The 242 transfer case features four ranges which give the Hummer the ability to tackle any terrain condition on or off-road.

When operating in high range, the internal differential allows the front and rear tires to rotate independently for smooth cornering on hard surfaces. The high lock and low lock ranges lock out the internal differential, transmitting power equally to the front and rear axles. The high lock position is used primarily on slippery surfaces such as snow-covered roads or muddy trails when added traction is needed. When operating in low lock, the transfer case provides an added gear reduction for increased torque. The low lock position is used under the most severe terrain conditions when both added traction and maximum power are required. The neutral position in the 242 transfer case allows the Hummer to be towed any distance without special preparation or fear of resulting damage to any drivetrain component.

The Hummer uses the General Motors Turbo Hydra-Matic 4L80 automatic transmission. The automatic transmission not only makes the Hummer easy to drive, it allows for a smooth transition of power for improved mobility off-road. The transmission offers three forward speeds and one reverse speed. Beginning with the 1992 and 1993 models, the Hummer 4L 80-E transmission offered four forward speeds and one reverse speed. The gear range can be selected manually for pulling heavy loads or operating in extremely difficult terrain conditions.

Another feature that makes the Hummer such a reliable vehicle is its cooling system. It actually has multiple cooling systems which service engine coolant, engine oil, transmission/transfer case oil, and power steering. This means that even in conditions of extreme heat or drivetrain stress, viscosity breakdowns are unlikely. In this picture, a number of Hummers are coming down AM General's production line. Due to a military requirement designed to keep the vehicle's height as low as possible in order to fit it into US military helicopters and cargo aircraft, the vehicle's radiator is set an angle.

75

Powering the civilian Hummer are two different types of General Motor's water-cooled V8 diesel engines (starting in 1995 a powerful gasoline engine was offered to buyers of civilian Hummers).

The diesel engine's durability and high-torque output allow the Hummer to negotiate the most difficult terrain with confidence. The diesel engine is also fuel efficient, giving the Hummer better fuel economy than many expect.

Additionally, the Hummer is equipped with variable-ratio power steering for fast, precise steering and handling.

The cooling of the V8 engine is handled by a large four-core, three inch thick radiator. Cooling is further enhanced by large oil coolers for the engine, transmission, transfer case, and power steering system.

The Hummer body is made of heat treated aluminum alloy that's tough, corrosion resistant, and very light. This light aluminum allows most of the Hummer's weight to be concentrated in the chassis and drivetrain components. Body panels are first bonded together using an epoxy adhesive, then riveted, which makes the Hummer's body extremely durable.

The design of the fuel system contributes to the Hummer's ability to climb and descend steep grades and operate on severe side slopes with minimum fuel in the twenty-five-gallon tank. A fuel/water separator ensures that clean fuel is always supplied to the V8 diesel. A dash-mounted indicator light lets the driver know of any fuel contamination.

The Hummer's exhaust system is low-restriction, high-flow exhaust. More importantly, components of the exhaust system are manufactured from stainless and aluminized steel, reducing corrosion to outlast conventional exhaust systems.

A central venting system equalizes the internal and external pressures of each of the major drivetrain components. A hose is connected to the vent on each component and leads to a central hose that connects to the air cleaner. This central vent system prevents water contamination of the components even when they are fully submerged.

The Hummer's body design also plays an important role in its unique capabilities. Built very much like an aircraft, the structural components of the all-aluminum body and body panels are first bonded together using an epoxy adhesive and then riveted, giving the Hummer body inherent strength and durability. This lightweight construction allows the bulk of the Hummer's weight to be concentrated in the chassis and heavy-duty drive-train components.

As for corrosion, aluminum gives the Hummer body a naturally high resistance to any type of corrosion, especially rust. Additionally, the hood is made of a fiberglass-reinforced composite that is virtually corrosion-resistant. And the roof and doors are made from two-sided galvanized steel, E-coated to resist corrosion.

The civilian Hummer is built in a modern facility dedicated exclusively to production of this versatile vehicle. Located in Mishawka, Indiana, near South Bend, the assembly plant is operated by AM General and features advanced tooling and assembly lines, state-of-the-art manufacturing technology, extensive use of robotics and computerization, and a sophisticated material handling process for parts and assemblies. AM General also has a one-mile test track adjacent to the plant to conduct road tests of new vehicles.

Military Hummer production began in January 1985, while civilian production began in late 1992. Approximately 1,000 people are employed in the plant, and some 500 suppliers providing over 3,000 parts. Hummer production contributes almost $40 million annually to the local economy.

The Hummer assembly plant incorporates proven procedures and systems of efficiency and quality. These include elimination of off-line repair stations and rapid defect feedback for on-line corrections, a test facility for actual test "dri-ving" in a ventilated block house with floor rollers before the vehicle leaves the assembly line, and expanded and refurbished assembly line work areas.

Improved manufacturing technology at the Hummer plant includes the use of robots for painting vehicles, and applying fillet welding to five major components of the Hummer chassis. While the body is in "white" production (before it is painted), automated drilling and riveting equipment is used extensively.

Every military and civilian Hummer that rolls off the assembly line must also pass an extensive series of checks by inspectors. AM General's goal has always been to produce a well-designed, well-engineered, thoroughly tested, and absolutely reliable vehicle.

Beside commercial fleet users of civilian Hummers, one of the most popular uses for the Hummer chassis has been as a fire-fighting vehicle. Be it forest, grass lands, freeways, airport, or multilevel parking decks when only a 4x4 vehicle can reach the scene, the Hummer is the perfect choice for any fire department. With more water carrying capacity than most mini-pumpers (up to 300 gallons of water) and unmatched off-road mobility, the Hummer can stand up to the most difficult conditions and provide a longer service life than any other existing 4x4 firefighting vehicle on today's market. *AM General*

CHAPTER 5

Hummer Off-Road Driving Tips

The condition and physical properties of terrain will affect the Hummer's performance. With proper driving techniques, the Hummer can overcome difficult terrain conditions and get you where you need to go.

Very important for every Hummer owner is to be familiar with the performance data of his or her vehicle. This will help you come to a better understanding of how and when to apply this information when operating the vehicle off-road.

Engine Performance

The Hummer has two torque curves if plotted on a graph. One is the available torque curve and the other is the net torque curve. The available torque curve is a constant curve, while the net torque curve is dynamic. The available torque curve is taken as the engine is out of the vehicle and connected to a dynamometer. The net torque output (290lb ft) is at peak at 1700rpm and declines thereafter.

The net torque curve represents the engine in the vehicle connected to the drivetrain and parasitic loads, such as the power steering pump, fan, alternator, etc., are attached. All of these accessories require engine power to operate. This takes away from the available engine torque. The net torque curve is an approximation if the accessory systems are under a load and driveline engaged. As the load on the accessories changes, the net torque will move between the two curve lines. Maximum efficiency of the engine is at 2000rpm. Although there is no tachometer on the Hummer, by listening to the engine you will be able to gauge engine rpm level quite well. The engine will tell you how hard it is working.

When driving off-road, you should operate the engine at no more than 1500 to 1600rpm. This will allow you to have reserve power if needed. If you are operating at 1700rpm or above and accelerate, you will be losing torque at the wheels.

Never drive your Hummer into any body of water at high speed. While it may sound like a great deal of fun. If any water surges over the top of the vehicle's hood and enters the engine it could cause serious damage if you try to start the engine without following the proper procedure. Always come to a complete stop before entering the water. When you enter the water don't drive more than 5mph. *AM General*

Gear Reduction

The amount of torque produced by only the engine of most vehicles is not enough to even turn the wheels of that vehicle! The additional necessary torque comes from gear reduction within the drivetrain (transmission, transfer case, etc.).

When a small gear drives a larger gear, speed is reduced, but the torque delivered by the larger gear is increased. The torque ratio between two meshing gears is directly related to the gear ratio of the driving to the driven gear. Thus, when a 12-tooth gear drives a 24-tooth gear, torque is

Despite its size and macho-looks, the civilian Hummer is easier to drive off-road then any other 4x4 vehicle. John Linarello, an AM General employee who instructs new Hummer dealers in driving the vehicle off-road at AM General's 400 acre test track center, describes his impressions of first-time drivers of the Hummer: "To my delight, I've found those drivers who have never driven an 4x4 vehicle make the best students. Because of the Hummer's outstanding off-road mobility, it only takes finesse to learn how to drive a Hummer." *AM General*

doubled; that is, the torque of the large gear is twice that of the small gear.

The maximum additive gear reduction in the Hummer is 35.36:1. This occurs when the transmission is in first gear (1) and the transfer case is in Low Lock (L) range. As the input changes, the output changes. Remember that at 1700rpm we get 290lb ft of torque. If we increase the rpm input, the rpm output will increase also. However, if we increase the rpm input over 1700rpm, the

According to John Linarello, "Many people who are used to driving the more typical light-weight civilian 4x4 off-road vehicles seem to think that they have to muscle the vehicle around in off-road conditions. They just can not believe that the Hummer has so much power and climbing ability and that muscling it isn't necessary. It always takes a while for them to relax and enjoy the vehicle's unmatched off-road ability." *AM General*

torque input is less, so that the torque output will be less, even though the rpm output is greater. The operator can change the gear reduction input and torque output by changing position of the transmission and transfer case levers. Also, the operator can change torque output by increasing or decreasing engine rpm.

Tire Loaded Radius

The tire loaded radius is the distance from the center of the axle to the tire point of contact with ground surface. A force line exists at the loaded radius. This force line is where maximum torque is applied from the axle, through the wheel and tire, to the ground surface. The tire loaded radius is reduced when the vehicle is loaded and/or tire pressure is reduced. This reduction in radius provides a mechanical advantage for the operation of the vehicle.

Also, when the tire pressure is reduced, the size of the tire footprint is increased, providing more traction between the tire and the ground surface.

The power of the civilian Hummer is well portrayed in this great shot of veteran racer Rod Hall's vehicle taking to the air during part of the 1993 Baja 1000 race. This grueling 501 mile cross-country race in Mexico's desert provided mile after mile of the toughest terrain on earth with which to test the Hummer. Rod Hall's Hummer finished first in its class, with a time of thirteen hours thirty-three minutes. Rod Hall operates a racing school out of the Reno, Nevada, area from mid-March through early November. *AM General*

Compared to older generations of light weight 4x4 vehicles with their very narrow wheelbases and dangerous tendencies to roll over when the going gets tough, the 6,000lb Hummer, with its extra-wide wheelbase and massive shock absorption capabilities, is a welcomed guest at most 4x4 off-road rallies. Its automatic transmission and power steering make it unusually easy to drive in terrain that would cause other 4x4 drivers to break out in cold sweats. *AM General*

This provides increased flotation, which is critical for successfully traversing soft soil surfaces.

CAUTION: Ground clearance of the vehicle is reduced whenever tire pressure is reduced.

Brake and Throttle Modulation: for Enhanced Mobility

The use of this technique will give the Hummer operator the ability to traverse challenging obstacles with more confidence, safety, and care to both the vehicle and the terrain. It allows the operator to gain control of the vehicle systems and place power and wheel torque where it is needed most. This is how it works:

For logs, walls, rocks, severe ditches, etc.

1. Bring the vehicle to a complete stop. Do not overspeed the engine.

2. Select the proper transmission and transfer case gear range; usually first gear, low range on the T-Case for such obstacles.

Available as a piece of optional equipment, the civilian Hummer can be fitted with an electrically-powered, remote-controlled Warn winch with has a 12,000lb capacity. Equipped with a winch, civilian owners of Hummers complain that they spend more time pulling other 4x4s out of trouble than actually doing their own thing during 4x4 rallies. *AM General*

3. If wheel spin-out is experienced, let up on the accelerator to slow the wheel spin-out.

4. Slowly, fully depress the brake pedal with your left foot so all wheel spin is halted.

5. With the brake still applied, start to accelerate. As the engine gains power from acceleration, gradually reduce the pressure applied to the brake. (You can "feel" torque being distributed to

Other options available to the Hummer owner who spends a lot of time off-road include the Brush guard, which helps protect the Hummer's hood, headlights, and radiator grilles from damage by branches, trees, and heavy brush. Also available for civilian Hummer owners are rocker panel shields which can protect the vehicle's aluminum body by absorbing and distributing the impact of rocks, boulders, logs, and other hostile terrain features. *AM General*

US military Hummers are not fitted with spare tires. Since they are all equipped with run flat tires, the US military believes that spare tires would take up too much room on the vehicle that could be used for more important items. Instead, supporting vehicles and repair teams are designated to replace Hummer tires. For civilian owners of Hummers not equipped with run flat tires, AM General offers a swing-away spare tire carrier as an option. It is mounted on the right-hand side of the Hummer's rear bumper. This convenient carrier swings clear to fully access the vehicle's cargo area. A bed mounted carrier is also available. *AM General*

the wheel that has the most traction as the vehicles starts to move.)

6. After the first wheel crosses the obstacle, be prepared to modulate the brake and throttle for the following wheels.

For mounds, washouts, loose up-hill slopes, ditches, etc.

When wheel spin-out occurs as the vehicle is moving, the operator will notice a slight shaking or shuddering of the vehicle. This is the indi-

When your going up hills in your Hummer don't drive blind. When you come to the top of a hill, slow down and be prepared to stop if necessary. There may be somebody else coming up the other side of the hill. Even worse, there may not be another side to the hill your climbing, just a cliff!

Police and sheriff's departments around the country have been taking a keen interest in the Hummer's potential for law enforcement. The Salt Lake Sheriff's Department has already added the Hummer to their inventory. *AM General*

cation that a loss of traction is occurring on this terrain. The operator should:

1. Assess the terrain properly and adjust vehicle speed and gear ranges accordingly; High-Lock position for higher speed, Low for more torque.

2. Apply slight pressure to the brake when the shuddering sensation is felt, keeping the vehicle moving at a constant speed.

3. Be prepared to modulate through the adverse terrain.

Practical Operation and Off-Road Techniques

Safety First. Safety of the operator, passengers, and equipment is of primary concern. Always wear your safety belt and insist that your passengers do too.

Protect the Environment. Remember that driving on public or private land is a privilege, not a right. Respect environmental rules for all areas in which you operate your Hummer.

Keep Control of your Hummer. Drive within your limitations and your vehicle's capabilities. The best way to keep control of your vehicle is to keep control of your speed. Use Low Lock (L) for slow speed and maximum control. Traveling at higher speeds gives less reaction time, less control, and the need for more braking distance. Accelerate slowly and smoothly. Use your transmission and transfer case to maintain engine rpm and vehicle momentum.

Know your Hummer. Perform all pre-operation and post-operation checks as stated in the Owner's Manual. Practice your driving skills and familiarize yourself with the Hummer on somewhat gentle terrain at first, gradually increasing in difficulty as your knowledge and abilities grow.

Pack Properly. When you are packing your Hummer, stow the heaviest items on the bottom and as far forward as possible. Tie down the cargo to keep it from shifting or being thrown around. Do not forget the off-highway necessities: water, first aid kit, recovery kit, fire extinguisher, tire pressure gauge, air compressor, tire repair kit, spare belts, hoses, and typical repair parts.

Know where you are going. Know the terrain and the weather you are likely to encounter. Acquire maps at camp offices or ranger stations when driving on public sites. Make sure your maps are up to date. If you plan to travel beyond walking distance from civilization, use the buddy plan: go in pairs. It is best if at least one of the vehicles has a winch big enough to pull either vehicle out of trouble. Citizen Band (CB) radios are extra safety factors.

Keep Your Driving Skills Sharp. The Hummer's unique design characteristics allows unparalleled approach angles and maneuvering capabilities. Be sure you are comfortable with handling the vehicle by practicing turning through pylons or other safe obstacles. There is very little body hangover ahead of the Hummer's front tires, so the front of the vehicle will react quicker than other vehicles when turning.

Work with Stability. Major contributing factors to the outstanding stability of the Hummer are its wheelbase and track width. When following tracks or trails of narrower vehicles, position the left wheels of the Hummer to the left of the other wheel tracks. In tight off-road situations, place the left side of the vehicle close to the obstacle, and ease through, noting clearance on the right. If there is any doubt of clearance, get out of the vehicle and check.

Be Aware of Changing Terrain. The terrain you are operating over is dynamic (changing every day), depending on climatic conditions. You must be aware of these changes, even if you are familiar with the surrounding terrain. Even the position of the sun in the sky will change the appearance of the terrain features. This is very evident in sandy areas. Different types of soils and soil conditions affect vehicle performance.

The operator must adapt his performance to these changing conditions so that maximum vehicle performance can be achieved.

Watch out for Other Vehicles. You will probably plan your trip with the hopes of having a remote area all to yourself. Other people are hoping the same thing. Mark and flag your Hummer for high visibility.

Watch out for Surprises! A sudden bump, ditch, or rock can make you lose control if you are

When going uphill in your Hummer, always select the proper transmission and transfer range before starting. Don't accelerate too quickly going up a hill as it could cause you to lose traction. At the same time you don't want to go to slow and loose the power you need to get up the hill. Try to maintain a constant speed and try to keep it smooth. *AM General*

not prepared. Use the transmission to regulate your speed. If you have to brake hard, you are probably driving too fast. Hitting a sharp bump or ditch with the brakes locked can cause serious damage to the vehicle.

Be Aware of Hidden Danger. In off-highway driving, keep alert for hidden obstacles. An innocent appearing clump of grass may, and often times will, conceal large rocks. Know your vehicle and be alert for changes in engine and tire

The Hummer was designed to drive through 30in of water. That being said, when you plan on crossing a body of water no matter how large or small, you better know how deep the water is. You also need to know the condition of the ground under the water. Thick mud or quicksand could cause problems for any Hummer owner. It is always better to be safe than sorry. *AM General*

sounds. Be ready to react to changing surface conditions.

Get a Grip — and Keep It. Keep a firm grip on the steering wheel when driving off-highway. Rocks, bumps, or ditches can jerk the steering wheel, making you lose control if you are not alert. Do not put your hands inside the steering wheel or on the spokes —a sharp jerk can cause serious injury.

"Read" the Terrain like an Expert. Know the type of terrain you are driving on and know how your Hummer reacts on this terrain. Watch out for changes in the terrain. Changes in the surface may effect stopping distance and acceleration or cause wheel spin or sliding sideways. If you question the terrain, walk the area before driving through.

Know How to Regain Control. If you encounter a vehicle control problem when making a turn, normally the best course of action is to accelerate gradually until you regain complete control.

Finish What you Start. Once you start an off-road maneuver do not stop or hesitate but follow through with the maneuver.

Side Slope Operation

Plan Every Move. Plan so you will not have to stop in a dangerous situation, such as on a hillside. If you have to stop on a hillside and have to get out of the vehicle, do so on the uphill side. A hole or a rut on the downhill side or a hump or a rock on the uphill side will make the Hummer tilt more and place you in a dangerous position.

Learn to Judge a Slide Slope. Remember, the Hummer is designed to go up or down at least a sixty percent slope and to traverse a forty percent side slope. The rule of thumb is: if you have any doubts, go around. If there is no way around, walk over it first to get a feel for the terrain.

Straight Ahead is Not Always Best. If you are driving on a side slope in loose sand or gravel or in mud, use the steering wheel to weave slightly back and forth (serpentine driving). Serpentine driving will help correct the vehicle's tendency for the rear end to drift down the slope. If the rear end of the vehicle does start to slip down slope, steer into the direction of the slip just as if you were driving on ice or another slippery surface.

Operation on Hills

Don't Drive Blind. When you come to the top of a blind hill, slow down and be prepared to stop if necessary. There may be something just over the crest that will cause serious problems.

Adjust Vehicle Speed. When going uphill, select the proper transmission and transfer ranges before starting. Keep it smooth and do not accelerate too quickly — this could cause you to lose traction. Maintain your speed.

Use the Drivetrain to Brake. When going downhill, use the engine compression, transmission and transfer case to control the speed. If you are in deep sand, do not use the brakes. Keep the speed down to where you can control the Hummer.

90 Degree Approach. As a rule, go straight up or down a hill. Avoid circumstances that may cause you to traverse a side slope.

Operation in Water

The Hummer is designed to drive through 30in (81cm) of water. When driving in water, make sure you know how deep it is and the condition of the road surface under the water. Stop. Enter the water slowly (not more than 3-5mph) to prevent water from surging over the top of the engine.

Should Water Get in the Engine. If the engine gets submerged, water could enter the engine and cause serious damage if you try to start the engine without following the proper procedure. First, pull or tow the vehicle to a dry, safe place, and then have a service technician do the following:

    a. Remove glow plugs.

    b. Drain and refill with new oil

The Hummer can get you places that no other 4x4 vehicle can. Before you start driving off-road to the places you have always dreamed of, you need to acquire certain skills to get there in a safe and sane manner. Know the type of terrain you will be driving on and how your Hummer reacts on that terrain. Watch out for changes in the terrain. Changes in the surface may effect stopping distance and acceleration. *AM General*

c. Clean air filter element and let dry.

d. Crank engine to force water out of cylinders through glow plug ports.

e. Reinstall glow plugs.

f. Restart engine.

Crossing Obstacles

Approach Angle: a Key to Mobility. If you encounter a large dip in the terrain, do not enter straight on — enter at an angle. For very large dips, ditches, or small washes, coast in, using the engine as brake, then, using the low ranges in the transmission and transfer case, power out.

Roll Your Tires Over Large Rocks. Do not straddle large rocks, drive over them letting the tire envelope the rock. Remember, the tread of the tire is thicker and tougher than the side wall of the tire and is more resilient to impact than underbody components.

Log Crossing. Using the proper technique, the Hummer will cross fairly large logs, up to 16in (40.6cm) in diameter. Approach the log at approximately a fifteen degree angle with the transfer case in "L" and "walk" the Hummer over one tire at a time. As with all obstacles, face tires perpendicular to the object for best traction and tire life. It may be necessary to modulate the brake pedal and accelerator to avoid spin-out. Ease the vehicle down from the log with your brake.

Operation in Sand

Adjust Tire Pressure for Sand Operations. Deflating the tires will give a larger load bearing surface, a bigger footprint, which will help you stay on top of the sand and will provide better traction. Do not deflate the tires below 12psi for extended periods. You may deflate down to 8psi for very short periods of time. The optional Central Tire Inflation system (CTI) will greatly enhance sand operations.

Use a Perpendicular Approach Both Ascending and Descending. Avoid going up or down at an angle. Sand dune slopes change constantly from wind and water erosion, so when you come to the top of a sand dune, stop and check the area before proceeding. There may be a large dip or other unforeseen obstacles that could cause serious problems. When driving down the face of a sand dune, use the cylinder compression of the engine, low transmission and transfer case range to control your speed: DO NOT USE YOUR BRAKES! Come straight down. When driving in soft sand try to stay out of ruts left by other vehicles

Using the Winch

Rigging a Winch the Right Way. A winch is a versatile and powerful addition to your Hummer. Think through your winching set-up before you flip the switch. Slopping rigging can result in serious injury to yourself or others as well as damage to your vehicle and equipment. Refer often to the winch manufacturer's operation handbook for detail instructions.

"Basic" Single-Line Rig. First, encircle your winch with a choker rope or nylon strap/tree trunk protector and attach the clevis where the loops come together, then hook the wire rope from the winch securely to the clevis. This method keeps the winch line absolutely straight, which is essential for maintaining the maximum tensile strength of the wire rope.

Always drape a blanket, coat, or chain over the wire rope as a damper in case of anchor failure.

"Snatch Block" or Double-Line Rig. By attaching a snatch block to your tree trunk protector or choker and then rigging your winch line through the snatch block and back to a solid mounting point on your vehicle, you give yourself a 2:1 mechanical advantage over single line pulling.

Even more significant, however, is that for a given load, the double line rig will allow the winch motor to turn faster and to draw less amperage than a single line rig. This means longer and heavier loads can be pulled without overheating the motor.

Directional or Angle-Pull Rig. A snatch block positioned midway along the winch line allows you to pull at sharp angles without compromising winch performance.

Returning to On-Road — A Checklist

Before returning to the highway, stop and check all items which can impact how your vehicle will get you home.

When driving your Hummer, roll your tires over large rocks, do not straddle them. Remember, the tread of the Hummer tire is thicker and tougher than the side wall of the tire and is more resilient to impact than the vehicle's underbody components.

The safest rule for off-road driving is always to travel with at least one other vehicle, that way there will always be somebody to bail you out in case of an emergency. *AM General*

— Clean all mud and debris from tires and underbody.

— Clean windows and mirrors for optimum visibility.

— Inspect and inflate all tires to proper levels for on-road driving.

— Inspect brake and air lines for leakage and hanging debris.

— Check that stowage tie downs are tight and cargo is secure.

— Check all fluid levels.

— Drive safely and enjoy your Hummer!

Rod Hall's Off-Road Driving School offers hands-on training to impart the skills needed to push a high-performance truck and driver to maximum potential. The school teaches basic techniques such as reading terrain, driving at speed in difficult situations, vehicle respect and proper use of the race environment. Some of Rod's current customers include the Chrysler Corporation, US Forest Service and even the US Marine Corps. *AM General*

Index